~A BINGO BOOK~

# Texas
# Bingo Book

## COMPLETE BINGO GAME IN A BOOK

## Written By Rebecca Stark

ISBN 978-0-87386-536-4

**Educational Books 'n' Bingo**

Printed in the U.S.A.

# TEXAS BINGO
## Directions

**INCLUDED:**

List of Terms

Templates for Additional Terms and Clues

2 Clues per Term

30 Unique Bingo Cards

Markers

1.  **Either cut apart the book or make copies of ALL the sheets. You might want to make an extra copy of the clue sheets to use for introduction and review. Keep the sheets in an envelope for easy reuse.**

2.  Cut apart the call cards with terms and clues.

3.  Pass out one bingo card per student. There are enough for a class of 30.

4.  Pass out markers. You may cut apart the markers included in this book or use any other small items of your choice.

5.  Decide whether or not you will require the entire card to be filled. Requiring the entire card to be filled provides a better review. However, if you have a short time to fill, you may prefer to have them do the just the border or some other format. Tell the class before you begin what is required.

6.  There are 50 topics. Read the list before you begin. If there are any topics that have not been covered in class, you may want to read to the students the topic and clues before you begin.

7.  There is a blank space in the middle of each card. You can instruct the students to use it as a free space or you can write in answers to cover topics not included. Of course, in this case you would create your own clues. (Templates provided.)

8.  Shuffle the cards and place them in a pile. Two or three clues are provided for each topic. If you plan to play the game with the same group more than once, you might want to choose a different clue for each game. If not, you may choose to use more than one clue.

9.  Be sure to keep the cards you have used for the present game in a separate pile. When a student calls, "Bingo," he or she will have to verify that the correct answers are on his or her card AND that the markers were placed in response to the proper questions. Pull out the cards that are on the student's card keeping them in the order they were used in the game. Read each clue as it was given and ask the student to identify the correct answer from his or her card.

10. If the student has the correct answers on the card AND has shown that they were marked in response to the *correct questions,* then that student is the winner and the game is over. If the student does not have the correct answers on the card OR he or she marked the answers in response to *the wrong questions,* then the game continues until there is a proper winner.

11. If you want to play again, reshuffle the cards and begin again.

**Have Fun!**

# TERMS INCLUDED

Alamo

Aquifer(s)

Armadillo

Austin

Stephen F. Austin

Balcones Escarpment

Barbed Wire

Basin and Range

Bluebonnet

Border

Caddo

Cattle

Central Plains

Chuck Wagon

Climate(s)

Coastal Plains

Comanche

Confederate States of America

Constitution

County (-ies)

Crop(s)

Dallas

Edwards Plateau

El Paso

Executive Branch

Geographic Regions

Guadalupe

High Plains

Horned Lizard

Houston

Sam Houston

Judicial Branch

Juneteenth

Legislative Branch

Lone Star

Missions

Monarch Butterfly

Oil

Panhandle

Quanah Parker

President(s)

Rangers

Republic of Texas

Rio Grande

San Antonio

Juan Seguín

Sheep

Texas Independence Day

Texas  Revolution

Treaty of Guadalupe Hidalgo

# Additional Terms

Choose as many additional terms as you would like and write them in the squares. Repeat each as desired.
Cut out the squares and randomly distribute them to the class.
Instruct the students to place their square on the center space of their card.

|  |  |  |  |  |
|---|---|---|---|---|
|  |  |  |  |  |
|  |  |  |  |  |
|  |  |  |  |  |
|  |  |  |  |  |
|  |  |  |  |  |
|  |  |  |  |  |

# Clues for Additional Terms

Write two clues for each of your additional terms.

| | |
|---|---|
| _____<br>1.<br><br>2. | _____<br>1.<br><br>2. |
| _____<br>1.<br><br>2. | _____<br>1.<br><br>2. |
| _____<br>1.<br><br>2. | _____<br>1.<br><br>2. |

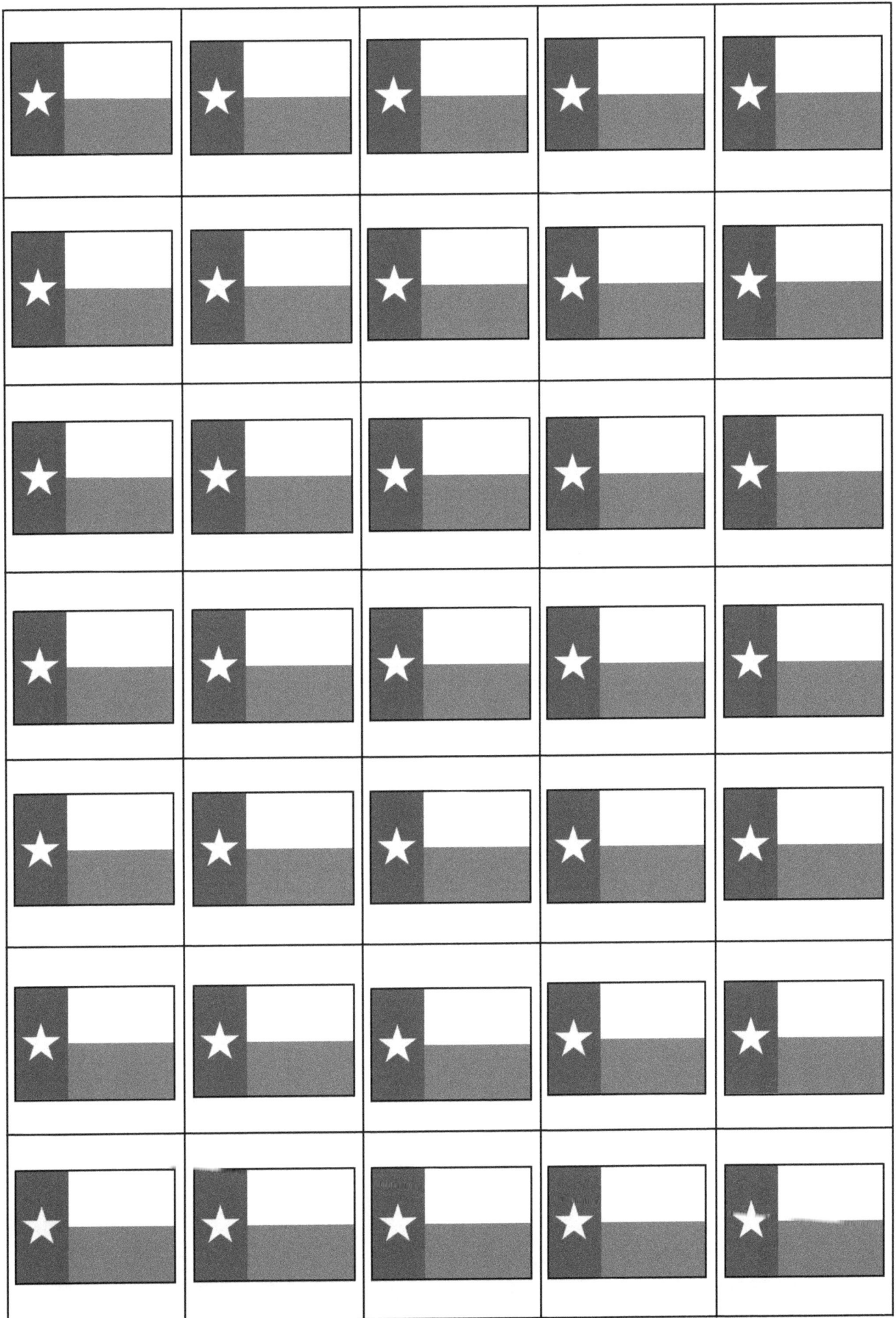

| | |
|---|---|
| **Alamo**<br>1. "Remember the ___" became a battle cry for future battles. All but two of the defenders of the ___ were killed.<br>2. Jim Bowie, Davy Crockett, and William Travis were among those who died defending the Alamo. | **Aquifer(s)**<br>1. ___ are underground layers of earth and rock that provide water for wells and irrigation.<br>2. The Southern High Plains is one of the richest areas in the state because of the Ogallalla ___ and the irrigation from it. |
| **Armadillo**<br>1. The nine-banded ___ is the state small mammal.<br>2. The ___ is the only mammal with a protective armored shell. | **Austin**<br>1. ___ is the capital of Texas. It is in the Coastal Plains region.<br>2. The capitol building in ___ is larger than that of any other state. |
| **Stephen F. Austin**<br>1. ___ established the first Anglo settlement in Texas. He became known as the "Father of Texas."<br>2. The capital of Texas is named for him. | **Balcones Escarpment**<br>1. The ___ is a geologic fault zone. Above the ___ are interior rolling plains. Below it are coastal plains.<br>2. The ___ separates the Edwards Plateau in the west from the Coastal Plains. |
| **Barbed Wire**<br>1. Before the invention of ___, livestock roamed freely.<br>2. ___ was invented by Joseph Glidden in 1853. Its use caused many disagreements between ranchers and farmers. | **Basin and Range**<br>1. The ___ Region is a very dry region in the westernmost part of the state. El Paso is in this region.<br>2. The ___ is the only mountainous region in Texas. The highest peak in Texas is here. |
| **Bluebonnet**<br>1. The ___ is the state flower.<br>2. Ennis is the official ___ city and trail.<br>The official ___ festival is the Chappell Hill ___ Festival held every April. | **Border**<br>1. Louisiana, Arkansas, Oklahoma, and New Mexico all ___ Texas.<br>2. Mexico and the Gulf of Mexico ___ Texas to the south. |

| | |
|---|---|
| **Caddo**<br>1. The ___ were Native American of East Texas. The name "Texas" comes from a ___ word.<br>2. The ___ Indians called their group of tribes the "Tejas," meaning "those who are friends." | **Cattle**<br>1. The largest source of agricultural revenue in Texas comes from the sale of beef ___.<br>2. Beef ___ are the most important livestock product. Others include broilers, or young chickens; dairy products; chicken eggs; and hogs. |
| **Central Plains**<br>1. The North ___ are part of the Central, or Interior, Lowlands. The region is divided into the West Texas Rolling Plains, Grand Prairie, and the Eastern and Western Cross Timbers.<br>2. Fort Worth and Abilene are in this region. | **Chuck Wagon**<br>1. The ___ is the state vehicle.<br>2. Texas rancher Charles Goodnight is credited with inventing the ___ to carry cowboys' food and supplies on trail drives. |
| **Climate(s)**<br>1. Due to its large size, Texas has several different ___.<br>2. Generally speaking, the ___ of the eastern half of Texas is humid subtropical. The western half is semi-arid with some arid regions. | **Coastal Plains**<br>1. About 1/3 of the state is in the Gulf ___. The region is characterized by low, flat land; some wooded areas; coastal sands; and many rivers. Austin, Houston, and San Antonio are in the ___.<br>2. Subregions of the ___ include Piney Woods, Post Oak Belt, Blackland Belt, Coastal Prairies, Lower Rio Grande Valley, and Rio Grande Plain. |
| **Comanche**<br>1. The ___ were exceptional horsemen. During much of the eighteenth and nineteenth centuries these Native Americans dominated the Southern Plains.<br>2. Quanah Parker was a ___ leader. | **Confederate States of America**<br>1. Texas was one of 11 states that seceded from the United States and joined the ___.<br>2. Jefferson Davis was President of the ___. |
| **Constitution**<br>1. The Constitution of 1876 has more than 470 amendments.<br>2. The Texas ___ has many amendments because the state has only those powers specifically granted to it. | **County (-ies)**<br>1. There are 254 ___ in Texas.<br>2. Harris ___ has the most residents. Loving ___ is the least populous. |

| | |
|---|---|
| **Crop(s)**<br>1. Cotton is the most important cash ___ in Texas, especially in the South Plains.<br>2. In addition to cotton, important ___ are greenhouse and nursery products, corn for grain, hay, wheat, sorghum grain, peanuts, rice, and cane for sugar. | **Dallas**<br>1. The ___-Fort Worth metropolitan area is the fourth largest in the United States and the largest in Texas.<br>2. White Rock Lake in east ___ was formed by damming White Rock Creek, a tributary of the Trinity River. The ___ Arboretum is on the lake. |
| **Edwards Plateau**<br>1. ___ is the southernmost area of the Great Plains. Hill Country is a popular name for the eastern portion.<br>2. The Texas Angora goat and mohair industry centers in the Rio Grande Plain and on the ___, which borders the Rio Grande Plain on the north. | **El Paso**<br>1. ___ is on the Rio Grande. It is surrounded by the Chihuahuan Desert, the easternmost section of the Basin and Range region.<br>2. This city is across the river from Ciudad Juárez in Mexico. |
| **Executive Branch**<br>1. The governor is head of the ___. The present-day head of this branch is [fill in].<br>2. The ___ includes the governor, lieutenant governor, attorney general, comptroller of public accounts, commissioner of the General Land Office, and commissioner of agriculture. | **Geographic Regions**<br>1. East to west the four main ___ are the Gulf Coastal Plains, the Central Plains, the Great Plains, and the Basin and Range.<br>2. The Great Plains is subdivided into these ___: the High Plains; the Edwards Plateau; and Llano Basin. |
| **Guadalupe**<br>1. The ___ Mountains are in west Texas. The highest point in the state is here.<br>2. The highest point in Texas is ___ Peak in the ___ Mountains. It has an elevation of 8,749 feet. | **High Plains**<br>1. The ___ in northwestern Texas is part of the Great Plains. Amarillo and Lubbock are in this region.<br>2.The Caprock Escarpment divides the ___ and the lower West Texas Rolling Plains. |
| **Horned Lizard**<br>1. The state reptile is the Texas ___.<br>2. When a ___ horned lizard feels threatened, it flattens and freezes in place, trying to blend with the ground. | **Houston**<br>1. NASA's Johnson Space Center is in ___.<br>2. ___ is the largest city in Texas. It was incorporated in 1837 and named after the man who was president of the Republic of Texas. |

Texas Bingo

| | |
|---|---|
| **Sam Houston**<br>1. ___ was the first and third president of the Republic of Texas.<br>2. ___ was governor of the state at the start of the Civil War. He was removed from office when he refused to swear loyalty to the Confederacy. | **Judicial Branch**<br>1. The ___ interprets what our laws mean and makes decisions about the laws and those who break them.<br>2. The ___ is made up of several courts, the highest of which is the state Supreme Court. |
| **Juneteenth**<br>1. This holiday originated in Galveston. It is also known as Emancipation Day.<br>2. ___ became a legal state holiday in 1980. It celebrates June 19, 1865, the day on which abolition was announced in the state. | **Legislative Branch**<br>1. The ___ is composed of a 31-member Senate and a 150-member House of Representatives.<br>2. The ___ makes the laws. |
| **Lone Star**<br>1. Texas is nicknamed the ___ State.<br>2. Texas is called the ___ because of its state flag with a single star. | **Missions**<br>1. Spanish ___ were established to convert the Native Americans to Christianity.<br>2. There were a total of 26 ___ established in Texas. The first was San Francisco de la Espada. |
| **Monarch Butterfly**<br>1. The ___ is the official state insect.<br>2. Both the caterpillar and adult ___ are brilliant in color as a warning to predators that they are poisonous. | **Oil**<br>1. The first ___ field was drilled near the town of Nacogdoches in 1866.<br>2. The ___ field discovered at Corsicana marked the start of the ___ boom in the state. |
| **Panhandle**<br>1. The ___ is a rectangular area bordered by New Mexico to the west and Oklahoma to the north and east.<br>2. The Texas ___ comprises the northern most 26 counties in the state. Palo Duro Canyon is in the ___. | **Quanah Parker**<br>1. ___ was a great Comanche leader.<br>2. His mother was a white woman who had been taken captive by the Comanche as a young girl. |

Texas Bingo

| **President(s)**<br>1. ___ Dwight D. Eisenhower and Lyndon Baines Johnson were both born in Texas.<br>2. Texan George H.W. Bush was the 41st ___. His son, George W., was the 43rd. | **Rangers**<br>1. The Texas ___ were first used in 1823 by Stephen Austin to protect the settlements against Indian attacks.<br>2. Stephen Austin organized a group of citizens to provide protection. He referred to them as ___ because they had to range over the entire country. |
|---|---|
| **Republic of Texas**<br>1. Texas was called the ___ when it was a sovereign nation.<br>2. The ___ was in existence from 1836 to 1845. It became the 28th state on December 29, 1845. | **Rio Grande**<br>1. The ___ runs along the border of Mexico and Texas. It is called Rio Bravo in Mexico.<br>2. The Lower ___ Valley is the only area in Texas where winter temperatures are mild enough to support citrus crops. The Upper ___ Valley consists of a narrow strip of irrigated land. |
| **San Antonio**<br>1. The Alamo is in this city.<br>2. ___ is a city in the Coastal Plain. River Walk is a popular attraction there. | **Juan Seguín**<br>1. ___ was a Tejano leader who fought on the side of the Texans against Santa Anna.<br>2. ___ did not die at the Alamo because he was sent by Colonel Travis to cross enemy lines to try to get help for those at the Alamo. |
| **Sheep**<br>1. Cattlemen and farmers did not get along with the ___ ranchers.<br>2. Cattlemen and farmers were angered because ___ grazed the grass too short and trampled the crops. | **Texas Independence Day**<br>1. ___ is celebrated on March 2.<br>2. This holiday commemorates the adoption of the Texas Declaration of Independence. |
| **Texas Revolution**<br>1. This war took place when Texas was part of Mexico. It was between Mexico and Toxians, Anglo-American residents of Texas.<br>2. It began with the Battle of Gonzales on October 2, 1835. It ended with the Battle of San Jacinto on April 21, 1836.<br><br>Texas Bingo | **Treaty of Guadalupe Hidalgo**<br>1. Under the terms of the ___, Mexico recognized the Rio Grande as the southern boundary of the United States.<br>2. The ___ ended the Mexican War. As a result Mexico ceded all claims to Texas.<br><br>© Barbara M. Peller |

# Texas Bingo

| Oil | Alamo | Armadillo | County (-ies) | Stephen F. Austin |
|---|---|---|---|---|
| Confederate States of America | Aquifer(s) | Texas Independence Day | Houston | President(s) |
| Sheep | Horned Lizard |  | Lone Star | Texas Revolution |
| Juan Seguín | Quanah Parker | San Antonio | High Plains | Judicial Branch |
| Legislative Branch | Edwards Plateau | Climate(s) | Republic of Texas | Geographic Regions |

Texas Bingo: Card No. 1

© Barbara M. Peller

# Texas Bingo

| | | | | |
|---|---|---|---|---|
| Juan Seguín | Sheep | Executive Branch | Panhandle | Guadalupe |
| Judicial Branch | Coastal Plains | Bluebonnet | Quanah Parker | Juneteenth |
| Caddo | Edwards Plateau | | El Paso | San Antonio |
| Missions | Monarch Butterfly | Horned Lizard | Treaty of Guadalupe Hidalgo | Stephen F. Austin |
| President(s) | Texas Independence Day | Climate(s) | Confederate States of America | Republic of Texas |

Texas Bingo: Card No. 2

# Texas Bingo

| Edwards Plateau | San Antonio | Coastal Plains | High Plains | Sheep |
|---|---|---|---|---|
| Judicial Branch | Aquifer(s) | Border | Alamo | Dallas |
| Quanah Parker | Texas Independence Day | | Juneteenth | Austin |
| Horned Lizard | Caddo | Legislative Branch | Missions | Executive Branch |
| Republic of Texas | Cattle | Climate(s) | Treaty of Guadalupe Hidalgo | Guadalupe |

Texas Bingo: Card No. 3

# Texas Bingo

| Horned Lizard | Juneteenth | Armadillo | Cattle | Guadalupe |
|---|---|---|---|---|
| Sam Houston | Basin and Range | Alamo | Panhandle | Sheep |
| Lone Star | Missions |  | Geographic Regions | County (-ies) |
| San Antonio | Aquifer(s) | Texas Independence Day | Climate(s) | Bluebonnet |
| Balcones Escarpment | President(s) | Barbed Wire | Republic of Texas | Texas Revolution |

Texas Bingo: Card No. 4

# Texas Bingo

| President(s) | Stephen F. Austin | Quanah Parker | Bluebonnet | Cattle |
|---|---|---|---|---|
| Sam Houston | San Antonio | Border | El Paso | Aquifer(s) |
| Armadillo | Texas Revolution | | Houston | Crop(s) |
| Geographic Regions | Guadalupe | Oil | Treaty of Guadalupe Hidalgo | Central Plains |
| Coastal Plains | Climate(s) | Sheep | Horned Lizard | Lone Star |

# Texas Bingo

| Austin | Juneteenth | Executive Branch | Guadalupe | Texas Revolution |
|---|---|---|---|---|
| High Plains | Quanah Parker | Central Plains | Alamo | Sheep |
| Panhandle | Balcones Escarpment |  | Basin and Range | El Paso |
| Climate(s) | Legislative Branch | Treaty of Guadalupe Hidalgo | Barbed Wire | Armadillo |
| Judicial Branoh | Bluebonnet | Oil | Lone Star | Comanche |

# Texas Bingo

| Oil | Juneteenth | Crop(s) | San Antonio | Coastal Plains |
|---|---|---|---|---|
| Judicial Branch | Guadalupe | Edwards Plateau | Aquifer(s) | Sam Houston |
| Texas Revolution | County (-ies) | | El Paso | Basin and Range |
| Horned Lizard | Missions | Border | Juan Seguín | Caddo |
| Climate(s) | Cattle | Treaty of Guadalupe Hidalgo | Barbed Wire | Austin |

# Texas Bingo

| Lone Star | Juneteenth | Constitution | High Plains | Basin and Range |
|---|---|---|---|---|
| Sam Houston | Armadillo | Panhandle | Texas Revolution | Bluebonnet |
| Comanche | Cattle |  | Guadalupe | Stephen F. Austin |
| Republic of Texas | Horned Lizard | Juan Seguín | Balcones Escarpment | Missions |
| Texas Independence Day | Climate(s) | Barbed Wire | Quanah Parker | Judicial Branch |

Texas Bingo: Card No. 8

# Texas Bingo

| Lone Star | Juneteenth | Constitution | High Plains | Basin and Range |
|---|---|---|---|---|
| Sam Houston | Armadillo | Panhandle | Texas Revolution | Bluebonnet |
| Comanche | Cattle | | Guadalupe | Stephen F. Austin |
| Republic of Texas | Horned Lizard | Juan Seguín | Balcones Escarpment | Missions |
| Texas Independence Day | Climate(s) | Barbed Wire | Quanah Parker | Judicial Branch |

Texas Bingo: Card No. 8

© Barbara M. Peller

# Texas Bingo

| El Paso | Coastal Plains | Edwards Plateau | Comanche | Cattle |
|---|---|---|---|---|
| Balcones Escarpment | Guadalupe | Lone Star | Quanah Parker | Juneteenth |
| Dallas | Oil | | Aquifer(s) | Constitution |
| Central Plains | Stephen F. Austin | Legislative Branch | Houston | Crop(s) |
| Missions | Treaty of Guadalupe Hidalgo | Border | Juan Seguín | Geographic Regions |

# Texas Bingo

| Juan Seguín | High Plains | Basin and Range | Panhandle | Comanche |
|---|---|---|---|---|
| Texas Revolution | Bluebonnet | Alamo | Aquifer(s) | Guadalupe |
| Cattle | Juneteenth | | County (-ies) | Caddo |
| Legislative Branch | Geographic Regions | Central Plains | Treaty of Guadalupe Hidalgo | Dallas |
| Border | Judicial Branch | Executive Branch | President(s) | Lone Star |

# Texas Bingo

| Austin | Juneteenth | Quanah Parker | Central Plains | Judicial Branch |
|---|---|---|---|---|
| Constitution | Dallas | Houston | El Paso | Alamo |
| Sam Houston | Guadalupe | | Executive Branch | Edwards Plateau |
| Border | Sheep | Treaty of Guadalupe Hidalgo | Cattle | Juan Seguín |
| Balcones Escarpment | Climate(s) | Oil | Barbed Wire | Coastal Plains |

# Texas Bingo

| Coastal Plains | Stephen F. Austin | Dallas | High Plains | El Paso |
|---|---|---|---|---|
| Edwards Plateau | Judicial Branch | Armadillo | Barbed Wire | Aquifer(s) |
| Oil | Crop(s) | | Texas Revolution | Panhandle |
| Climate(s) | Missions | Guadalupe | Juan Seguín | Sam Houston |
| Juneteenth | Constitution | Cattle | Balcones Escarpment | Bluebonnet |

# Texas Bingo

| Central Plains | Stephen F. Austin | Austin | Dallas | Texas Revolution |
|---|---|---|---|---|
| Armadillo | Constitution | Guadalupe | El Paso | Caddo |
| High Plains | Bluebonnet |  | Edwards Plateau | Crop(s) |
| Lone Star | Treaty of Guadalupe Hidalgo | Basin and Range | Cattle | Juan Seguín |
| Climate(s) | Geographic Regions | Barbed Wire | Oil | Houston |

# Texas Bingo

| | | | | |
|---|---|---|---|---|
| Confederate States of America | Guadalupe | Quanah Parker | El Paso | Balcones Escarpment |
| Bluebonnet | Oil | Dallas | Aquifer(s) | Juneteenth |
| Central Plains | County (-ies) | | Executive Branch | Border |
| Geographic Regions | Treaty of Guadalupe Hidalgo | Cattle | Basin and Range | Austin |
| Climate(s) | Panhandle | Caddo | Judicial Branch | Lone Star |

Texas Bingo: Card No. 14

# Texas Bingo

| Houston | El Paso | Quanah Parker | Coastal Plains | High Plains |
|---|---|---|---|---|
| Austin | Executive Branch | Alamo | Armadillo | Balcones Escarpment |
| Texas Revolution | Oil | | Sheep | Juneteenth |
| Climate(s) | Dallas | Constitution | Treaty of Guadalupe Hidalgo | Central Plains |
| Judicial Branch | Missions | Barbed Wire | Comanche | Edwards Plateau |

# Texas Bingo

| Basin and Range | Dallas | Constitution | Comanche | Monarch Butterfly |
|---|---|---|---|---|
| Panhandle | Caddo | Crop(s) | Sam Houston | County (-ies) |
| Central Plainss | Stephen F. Austin |  | Texas Revolution | Edwards Plateau |
| Horned Lizard | Bluebonnet | Climate(s) | Houston | Juan Seguín |
| Balcones Escarpment | Rio Grande | Barbed Wire | Missions | Juneteenth |

# Texas Bingo

| Border | Rangers | Chuck Wagon | Dallas | Confederate States of America |
|---|---|---|---|---|
| Houston | Balcones Escarpment | Treaty of Guadalupe Hidalgo | County (-ies) | Crop(s) |
| El Paso | Lone Star | | Rio Grande | Constitution |
| Geographic Regions | Judicial Branch | Juan Seguín | Quanah Parker | Caddo |
| Legislative Branch | Central Plains | Coastal Plains | High Plains | Stephen F. Austin |

# Texas Bingo

| Comanche | Cattle | Bluebonnet | Central Plains | Panhandle |
|---|---|---|---|---|
| Juneteenth | Border | Legislative Branch | Texas Revolution | Balcones Escarpment |
| El Paso | Caddo | | Chuck Wagon | Armadillo |
| Stephen F. Austin | Alamo | Treaty of Guadalupe Hidalgo | Juan Seguín | Executive Branch |
| Rio Grande | Dallas | Quanah Parker | Rangers | Austin |

# Texas Bingo

| Texas Revolution | Austin | Dallas | Constitution | Juan Seguín |
|---|---|---|---|---|
| Houston | High Plains | Juneteenth | Coastal Plains | County (-ies) |
| Rangers | Cattle | | Aquifer(s) | Sheep |
| Executive Branch | Rio Grande | Legislative Branch | Missions | Chuck Wagon |
| Armadillo | Monarch Butterfly | Judicial Branch | Lone Star | Barbed Wire |

Texas Bingo: Card No. 19

# Texas Bingo

| Confederate States of America | Rangers | High Plains | Dallas | Barbed Wire |
|---|---|---|---|---|
| Bluebonnet | Edwards Plateau | Sam Houston | Legislative Branch | Panhandle |
| Stephen F. Austin | Crop(s) | | Horned Lizard | Alamo |
| President(s) | Texas Independence Day | Republic of Texas | Missions | Rio Grande |
| San Antonio | Lone Star | Monarch Butterfly | Juan Seguín | Chuck Wagon |

Texas Bingo: Card No. 20

# Texas
# Bingo

| Houston | Austin | Sam Houston | Dallas | President(s) |
|---|---|---|---|---|
| Stephen F. Austin | Chuck Wagon | Basin and Range | Constitution | Oil |
| Caddo | Judicial Branch | | Rangers | Quanah Parker |
| Legislative Branch | Coastal Plains | Rio Grande | Geographic Regions | Lone Star |
| Horned Lizard | Monarch Butterfly | Barbed Wire | Border | Missions |

Texas Bingo: Card No. 21

# Texas Bingo

| Comanche | Executive Branch | Chuck Wagon | Armadillo | Central Plains |
|---|---|---|---|---|
| Panhandle | High Plains | Sheep | Constitution | Aquifer(s) |
| Bluebonnet | County (-ies) | | Oil | Crop(s) |
| Rio Grande | Geographic Regions | Missions | Alamo | Sam Houston |
| Monarch Butterfly | Border | Rangers | Caddo | Horned Lizard |

# Texas Bingo

| Basin and Range | Rangers | Coastal Plains | Armadillo | Barbed Wire |
|---|---|---|---|---|
| Austin | Confederate States of America | Judicial Branch | Houston | Alamo |
| Executive Branch | Central Plains | | Republic of Texas | Oil |
| Caddo | Monarch Butterfly | Rio Grande | Border | Missions |
| President(s) | Texas Independence Day | Lone Star | Legislative Branch | Chuck Wagon |

Texas Bingo: Card No. 23

# Texas Bingo

| Basin and Range | Lone Star | Confederate States of America | Rangers | Constitution |
|---|---|---|---|---|
| Chuck Wagon | Barbed Wire | Sam Houston | Panhandle | Oil |
| Crop(s) | Comanche |  | Central Plains | Caddo |
| President(s) | Republic of Texas | Rio Grande | Border | Stephen F. Austin |
| San Antonio | Horned Lizard | Monarch Butterfly | High Plains | Texas Independence Day |

# Texas Bingo

| Horned Lizard | Sam Houston | Rangers | Quanah Parker | Chuck Wagon |
|---|---|---|---|---|
| Alamo | Stephen F. Austin | Houston | Basin and Range | Aquifer(s) |
| Geographic Regions | Constitution | | Republic of Texas | Rio Grande |
| Sheep | President(s) | Texas Independence Day | Monarch Butterfly | County (-ies) |
| Barbed Wire | Confederate States of America | Bluebonnet | Balcones Escarpment | San Antonio |

Texas Bingo: Card No. 25

# Texas Bingo

| Chuck Wagon | Rangers | Executive Branch | Panhandle | Comanche |
|---|---|---|---|---|
| Legislative Branch | High Plains | Constitution | Confederate States of America | Basin and Range |
| Geographic Regions | Republic of Texas | | County (-ies) | Horned Lizard |
| Border | Armadillo | President(s) | Monarch Butterfly | Rio Grande |
| Crop(s) | Balcones Escarpment | Quanah Parker | Texas Independence Day | San Antonio |

Texas Bingo: Card No. 26

# Texas Bingo

| | | | | |
|---|---|---|---|---|
| Executive Branch | Bluebonnet | Rangers | Confederate States of America | Edwards Plateau |
| President(s) | Republic of Texas | Houston | Rio Grande | Aquifer(s) |
| Treaty of Guadalupe Hidalgo | Texas Independence Day | | Monarch Butterfly | Horned Lizard |
| Comanche | Austin | Sam Houston | San Antonio | Alamo |
| Balcones Escarpment | County (-ies) | Chuck Wagon | Sheep | Crop(s) |

# Texas Bingo

| Executive Branch | Confederate States of America | Sheep | Rangers | Basin and Range |
|---|---|---|---|---|
| Edwards Plateau | Chuck Wagon | Republic of Texas | Panhandle | County (-ies) |
| Texas Independence Day | Caddo | | Crop(s) | Legislative Branch |
| Juan Seguín | Comanche | Judicial Branch | Monarch Butterfly | Rio Grande |
| Armadillo | El Paso | Balcones Escarpment | San Antonio | President(s) |

# Texas Bingo

| | | | | |
|---|---|---|---|---|
| Chuck Wagon | Confederate States of America | Comanche | Houston | El Paso |
| Missions | Legislative Branch | Sam Houston | Crop(s) | Sheep |
| Geographic Regions | Republic of Texas | | Aquifer(s) | Rangers |
| Edwards Plateau | President(s) | Guadalupe | Monarch Butterfly | Rio Grande |
| Basin and Range | Constitution | San Antonio | Austin | Texas Independence Day |

# Texas Bingo

| Cattle | Rangers | Panhandle | El Paso | Rio Grande |
|---|---|---|---|---|
| Alamo | Confederate States of America | Executive Branch | County (-ies) | Aquifer(s) |
| Geographic Regions | Central Plains | | Crop(s) | Sam Houston |
| San Antonio | Austin | Armadillo | Monarch Butterfly | Republic of Texas |
| President(s) | Texas Revolution | Texas Independence Day | Chuck Wagon | Sheep |

Texas Bingo: Card No. 30

www.ingramcontent.com/pod-product-compliance
Lightning Source LLC
LaVergne TN
LVHW061339060426

835511LV00014B/2005